The Collectibles

Tales of Love and Heartbreak

Komal Grover

Made with ♥ on the Notion Press Platform
www.notionpress.com

You broke my heart a thousand times
Into a million pieces
Yet when you walk through that door
I turn back to see you
Yet when you walk past me
My heart races ahead of time
Yet when you don't look at me
I want to hold you
Look into your eyes
Cry to sleep in your arms
And never wake up
To face the reality again!

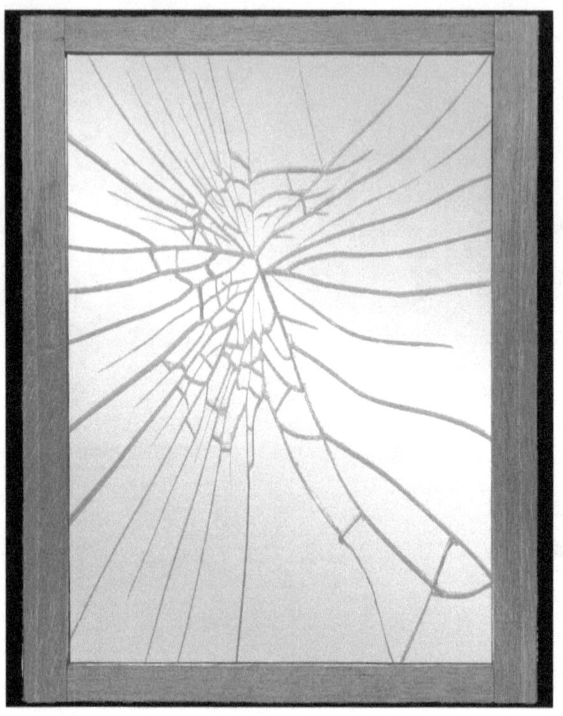

I know I mean nothing to you
Maybe just an escape
Maybe just an option
But to me you mean the world
A world that doesn't belong to me
A world that feels far out of reach
A world I wish was mine
A world I wish I could fit in
A world I see through the glass door
While the glass crashes my dreams
And me into a zillion pieces
And you disappear into the pieces
Leaving me broken forever

I wish I never found you
I wish I never loved you
I wish I never had you
And when I did, I wish I never lost you

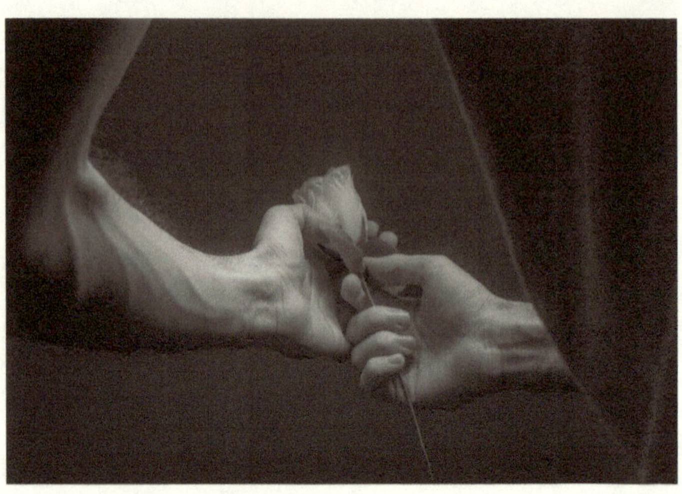

Will you find such love again?
If you do, I'd be happy for you
If you don't, will you think of me?
Will you see the moon and remember me, like I do?
Will you walk the paths we walked together and wish
I was there, like I do?
Will you see your hand and wish I could hold it, like I do?
Will a song remind you of me?
Will you ever love me like I do?

Was a just an object to you?
Was there never any love?
Was there no feeling at all?
Were your eyes lying all throughout?
Did you mean anything that you ever said to me?
Will my poetry just be a collectible to you, like my love is?

I wish I wasn't so stupid in love
I wish I didn't fall for your words
But if I didn't, would I know the kind of love I'm capable of?
With nothing in return and giving you my all,
Knowing I'll never be the same again yet loving you with all my heart, over and over again
Only to have you step on it all over again

What would it take for you to love me?
I wish I knew
I wish you told me
I would move the mountains to see you once
Burn the world to get into your arms
And die to stay there forever

Will you cry when I die?
Will you come to see me one last time?
Will you touch me the way you did?
Well, don't, I may come back to life
And you may walk away again
Leaving me alive and lifeless, yet again

Will this pain ever go away?
Will my eyes ever stop looking for you in the crowd?
Will my heart ever stop racing at your thought?
Will my feet ever stop walking towards you?
Will I ever stop loving you?

My poetry for you,
My love for you,
My heartbeat for you,
My smile for you,
My tears for you,
My pain for you,
My happiness for you,
Did it ever mean anything to you?

Was my love not enough for you?
What more did you want?

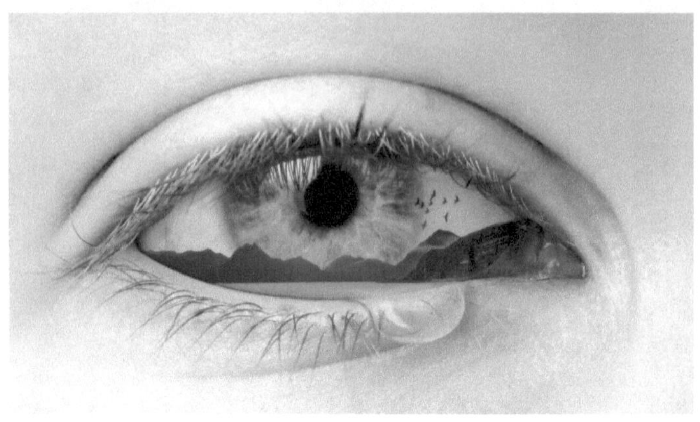

Will you hold my hand again?
Will you take me along into your world?
Will you walk this path with me?
Will you look into my eyes once more?
Will you stay this time?

Do you know how it feels to love and not be loved?
To cry and not show you my tears
To pray for you and not let you know
To miss you and not tell you
To write you and not make you read

That day, you held me and told me you want to take away
all my pain,
The next day, you held me and told me we can't be
together, giving me pain enough for a Lifetime

I will let you walk all over me a zillion times
Until one day when I won't

How do you feel
Shattering me over and over again
Do you feel good about yourself
Seeing me lost
Struggling to breathe
Dying to be in your arms again

You are not special
My love has made you special
Put you on a pedestal
And gave you my heart
Only for you to crush it
Wait till I put back the pieces together
And let you crush it once more

The sleepless nights
The sinking feeling
Will you ever know how much I love you?
Every time you did not look at me
Every time that you did not talk to me
My heart cried and feet trembled
I wish I could tell you how much I miss you
You left me drowning
And I'm still finding my way back up

Come back once
And don't go away
Stay
I'm an empty home without you

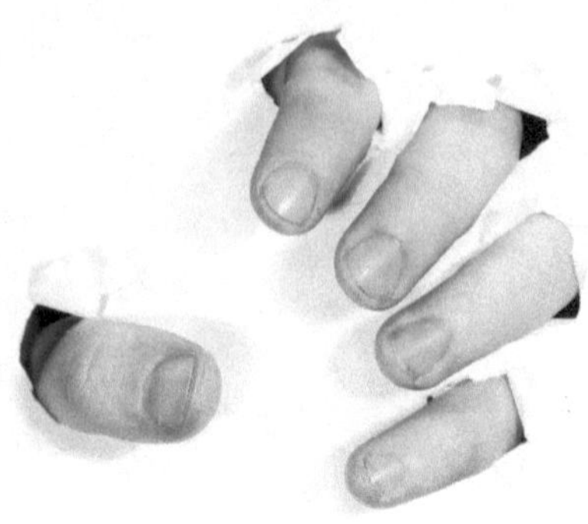

I have loved before
Cried before
But the love I feel for you is nothing what I've felt before
I daydream of you, all day
And hear your voice in my head
But you don't talk to me now
And your silence is killing me
I now know what a heartbreak truly is

Every moment spent with you
Every word you said to me
Fresh in my mind
Do you remember any of it?
Or was it all just a facade?

I haven't got out of the bed in days
Lying motionless
I keep looking at your pictures – I only have a couple of them
Tears have stopped rolling
But I haven't slept
Nor eaten
Hands shivering
Feet numb
I feel weak in the knees
Breathing seems difficult
Will you come back and hold me once?
For your touch is medicine to my body and life to my soul

It's December
The year is ending
The night is cold
And you're not here to hold me
'Tis the season
I waited for you
But you did not come
Wait until I die
For I shall then be as cold as you

Falling in Love makes you a poet
Heartbreak turns you into an artist

I keep going back to your city
and pass by your house everyday
Looking for you
Days go by
Without your sight
Dry and barren
Is my heart without you
And when I finally see you
I know
My place is in your arms
Where I shall never be

I lost my pride in your love
I lost my heart in your eyes
I lost myself in your arms
I loose myself everyday now loving you, looking for you

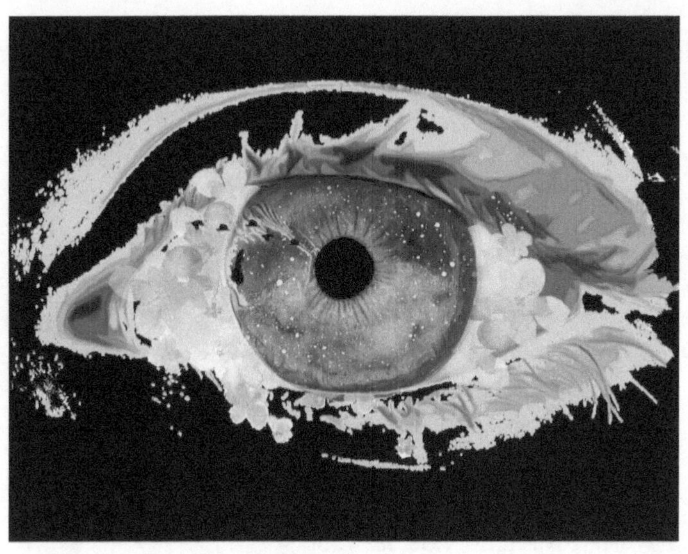

You're the master of my heart
Tuning my days and nights at your will
You're the master of all the lies
Killing me with your eyes
I laugh at your lies
And yet fall for you
For your eyes and lies are as pretty as you

My heart was empty before you
My dreams were empty before you
You came in and filled it with so much color
Only to leave it emptier than ever before
My heart has nothing to do now
And dreams have nowhere to go

It's so long since I have seen you – thirty-two days to
be precise
The longest I've been away from you – and your fragrance
around me
And I hope this remains the longest
I count every single day
How long till I see you again?
I have forgotten how to smile
But I remember your smile
And I remember your laugh
And your kiss
And your hug
Tonight my soul is longing for you
Why don't you come back

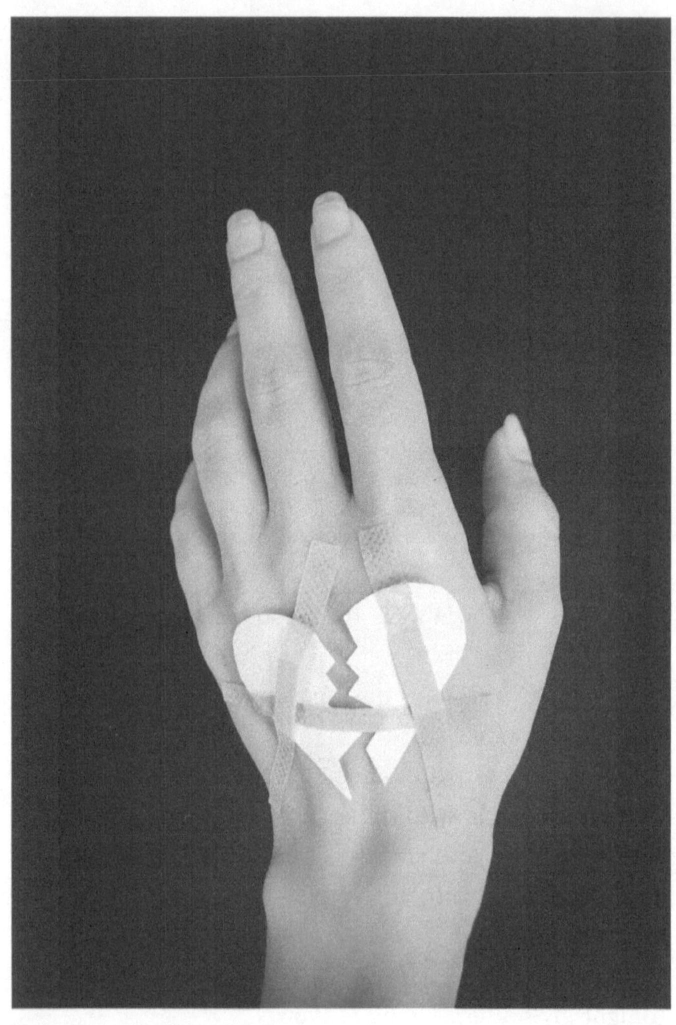

I wish you did not make those empty promises
I was empty before you
But your words gave me hope
And when you broke that hope
You broke me
Like never before

I don't know when did I start loving you
Maybe the day you held my face in your palms
Looked into my eyes
And kissed my forehead
Or the day you kissed my shoulder from behind
Or the day you fell asleep in my arms
And I kept watching you until the sunlight kissed open your eyes
Or the day I held your hand before closing my eyes and you held it more firmly with both your hands
Looking into my eyes

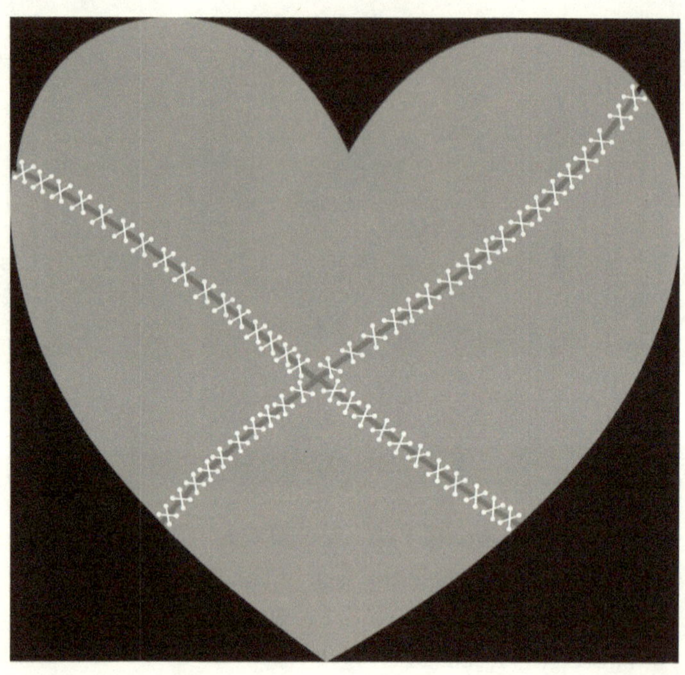

O love of my mine
Come here
See what I found
My heart laying in your closet, saying it will choose you
over and over again
"After all of this?" asked the closet
"Every single time" my heart answered in a beat
Such is the love you've made me fall in

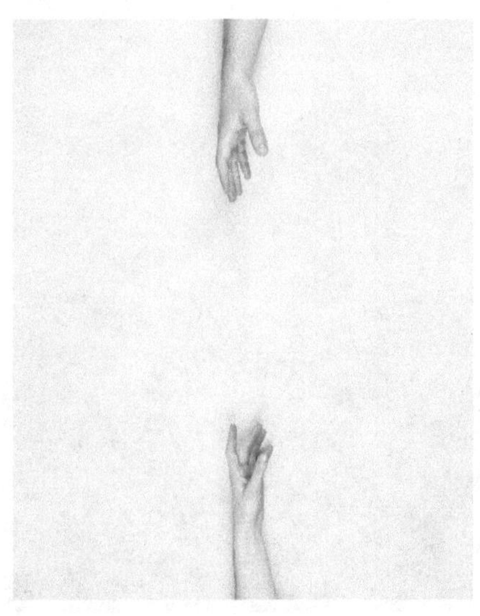

Grief is the price I paid to love you
And I will carry this grief to my grave
But I shall now let you go my love
Wishing you all the happiness that this world has to offer
Knowing you lied to me
Knowing your actions were all a farce
But loving you will always be the best feeling for me
For I loved you without any boundaries
And it was never love to you
So you never came back
And it was always love to me
Hence, I let you go
You may find love again
And I hope you do
But for me this will be the epitome of love
For I know not any greater form of love than this
And know that I will keep loving you forever and always
For I know not which one's more

In this world of gadgets, you're my book
Let me read you
Page by page
Let me go slow
For I never want to get to the end of this book

This first flight journey after this crazy love I fell in
Feels so different from all the previous ones
Leaving the city while you're in it
Knowing I will see you again
But not knowing when
Knowing you're down there somewhere
I keep seeing the city from the window
Until the concrete jungle
Gets lost from my sight
But your thoughts stay in my head
Like you stay in my heart

Every day I wake up
Starting the day thinking of you
Getting ready for you
Waiting for you
You don't come
My eyes keep looking for you
Every day I sleep
Thinking of you
And every day I dream
Of you coming to me
And I now love these dreams more than I love you
For that's the only time you choose me

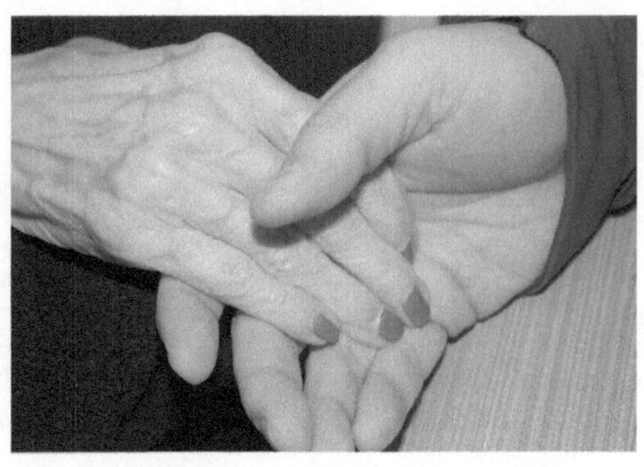

I want to see the rest of my sunsets with you
I want to dance under the moonlight with you
I want to lay under the stars with you
I want to keep gazing at you under the cold starry night
I want to see the shooting star with you
I want to kiss you under the first ray of sunlight that falls
on your cheek
I want to walk on the fresh snow with you with your
hands in mine
I want to get drenched with you in the rain
I want to hear the beach waves with you
I want to swim the cold-water lakes with you
I want to scale the mountains with you
I want to walk the grass with you, barefoot
I want to see the blooming flowers with you
I want to listen to old songs with you
I want to hear the birds chirping with you
I want to see the world with you
I want to laugh with you
Eat with you
Just be with you
Get wrinkled with you

Take me
Take me away
In your arms
For that's where I belong
Let me see the world through your eyes
And let me get lost in your words again

Do my poems sound incomplete?
Cause that's what I am, without you

Let me sleep in your arms one last time
Let me hold your hand one last time
Let me look into your eyes one last time
Let me kiss you one last time
Let me bury my head in your chest and cry one last time
let me love you one last time
Let me breathe with you one last time
Let me live one last time

I have nothing to give you
Except for this crazy love of mine
And I have nothing to ask of you
Except that you love me once

You remember the day I opened the house door to you
How I wish that happens everyday
you come home to me
And I open the door to you
And hug you before you enter the house
ask you about your day
And listen to you
Looking into your eyes
Every single time
Every single day
Forever

If there's only one house I could build in this lifetime,
I want it to be ours

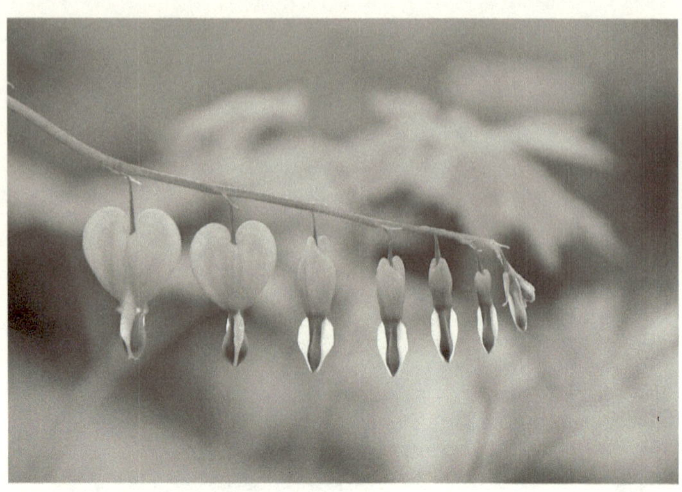

You didn't love me back
Yet I love you like this
What if you loved me
Even a fraction of what I do
I don't know how much more would I love you then

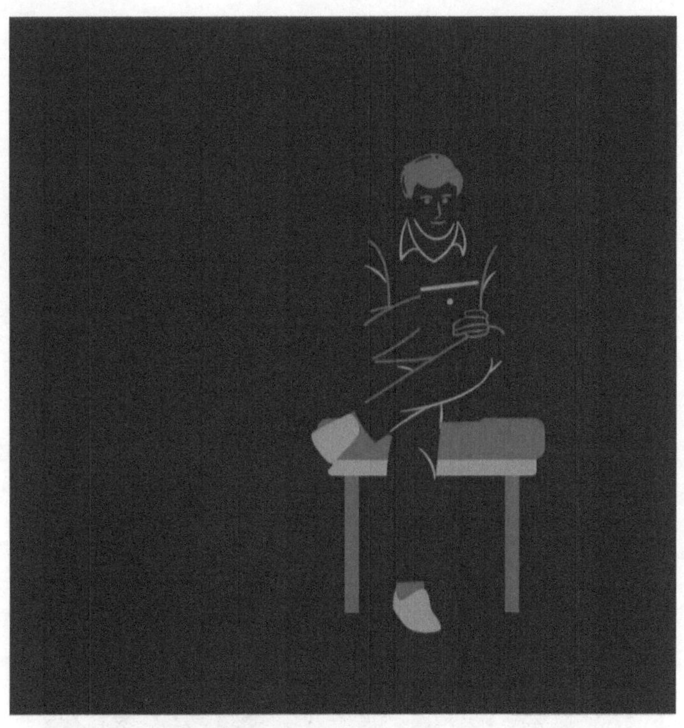

Will you show my poems to the world?
What will you tell them?
Will you tell them I wrote this for you?
Will you be happy about it?
Or will you mock me for my love?
Do as you wish
Whatever makes you happy
For your happiness is what matters to me

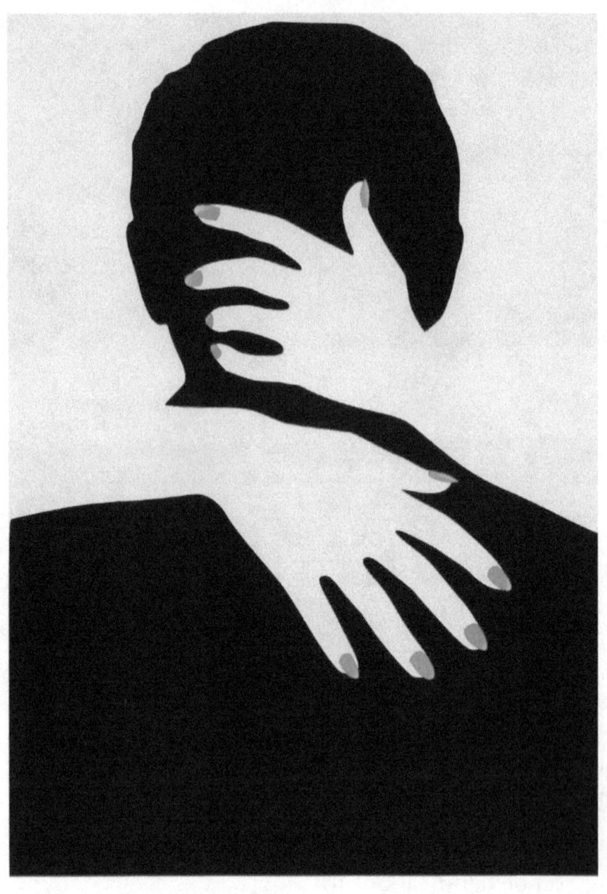

You know I love your tender lips
and your charming smile
and your melodious laugh
and your deep eyes
and your messed hair
and your gentle hands
and your slender neck
and your delicate ears
O I just realized I love the whole of you

I have said enough about my love for you
Now let me rest
Let me sleep
And don't wake me up
I'm going to meet you in my dreams
Let me stay there
Let me be happy for once
And who said it's just a dream
It's better than my reality
For I see you there everyday

I waited for him for days
And he just walked past me like a stranger
Without looking at me
Tears haven't stopped since then
Maybe something is bothering him
Or he would at least stop to smile
No, he is not heartless
Maybe he is hurt
I haven't heard him laugh in a while
I wish he told me what is hurting him
I will do everything to make him smile again
To get back the sound of his laugh

Is there something bothering you
Come talk to me
I'm here for you
Same place where you left me
I will listen to you without any conditions
And be there for you always

Words are my only way of expressing love
Words are my only way of healing
So whether you love me or break me
I will continue to write you

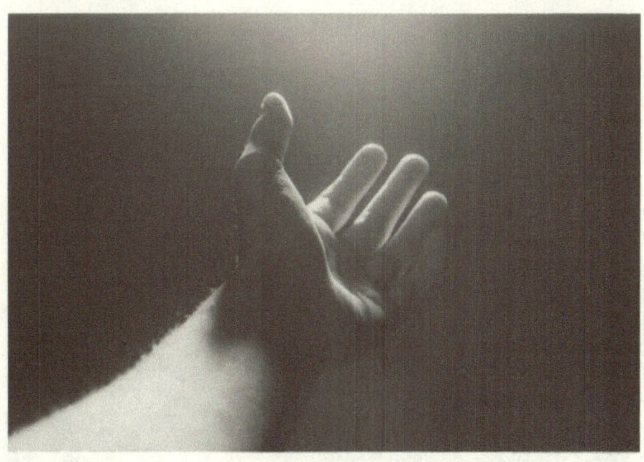

There are things I wanted to show you
stories I wanted to share with you
songs I wanted to listen with you
Memories I wanted to create with you
Experiences I wanted to enjoy with you
I'm keeping it all to myself now
For my mind knows I may now not be able to do any of it
But my heart doesn't want to accept – the thought of you
not being with me anymore
Why did I love you so much
And when I did, why did you not love me back
I'm weeping at this thought now
Telling myself I'll be okay
But I know I shall never be truly fine
You shall always ponder in my mind
live in my heart
And peep in my dreams
I will always think of what you're doing
Will you ever think of me?
So many unsaid things between us
Will we ever be able to communicate them?

My poetry is a testament of my love for you
Don't know what you'd make of it
And how you'd remember me
And if you'd ever remember me
But remember if you will, remember me as someone who loved you with all her heart
And still does
And misses you so much every single day
And would still give away the world to be with you

I know you're this quiet private person
not showing your feelings to the world
Loving and grieving in private
Whereas I may grieve in private
But when I love
I want to tell the world
And tell you from the top of the mountain
How much I love you
And that you mean the world to me

Do you know the void you leave in my heart, O my love,
every time you leave?
Cry not my heart, maybe we will see him tomorrow again,
or maybe not?
Or maybe the day after that?
Your absence drills my heart
And this is the only hope that keeps me alive

A broken heart
A lifeless soul
I loved so hard
He'll never know
He was an arduous lesson I wanted to be love
I tried so hard but how can I forget him
After all that he said
How can I stop loving him
After the hand he held and the lips he kissed

I will let you go in this lifetime
Only to have you in every other lifetime

I will find you
On the other side
O love
Beyond the rain and the sunshine
Beyond the waves and the moon
Beyond the world boundaries
Beyond the societal norms
Beyond your pride
Beyond my words

And then I shall have you
Completely to myself
Not sharing you with this world again
And Not letting you go away
Ever again

Why do I live
This life without you
Give me a reason to smile
The way you occasionally show up
Make it a permanent affair

An artist lives through his art
Long after he's gone
My love for you will live through my poetry
Long after you've destroyed me
And my lips will remember your name
Till they're permanently sealed

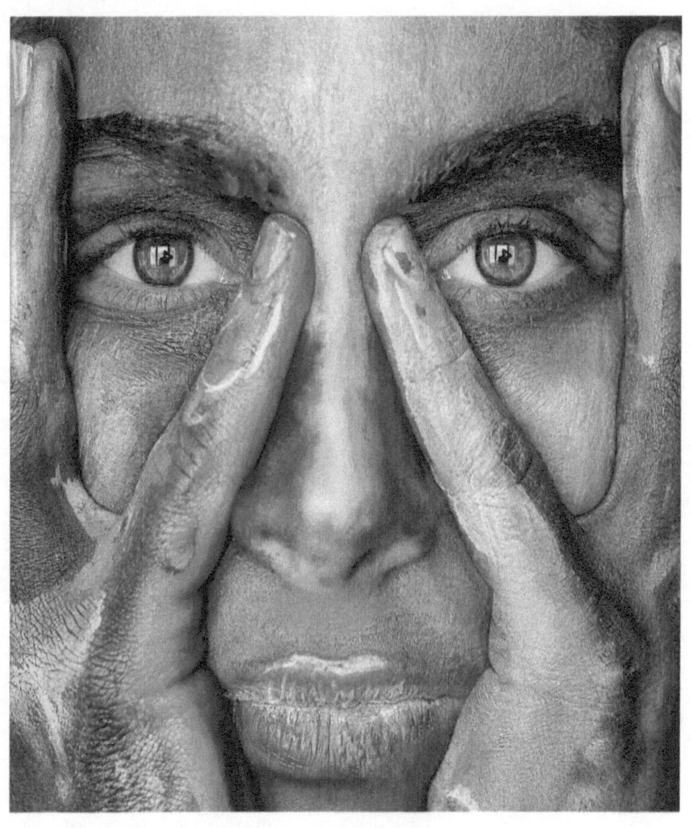

You, are my deepest desire
And my darkest truth
My sincerest love
And my most treasured memory

Some days I just want to come running to you
And find my solace in your arms
Feel your breath and hear your heartbeat
But I stop myself
For this distance that you have created
Has left me feeling unwanted and crushed

I can never say goodbye to you
What is good about leaving you
Even if for a short while
I don't need this distance from you

You are the city I want to thrive in
You're the house I want to flourish in
But I will now neither thrive nor flourish
For You, are not mine

I always miss you
When I see the moon above
The moon keeps fading
And then vanishes
Every fortnight
But my love for you neither fades nor vanishes
It stays the same
Till the moon comes back in all its glory
And I miss you all over again

You've given me love enough for this lifetime
But for every other lifetime, I want you, along with this love

Mornings bring hope
Of seeing you
The Noons bring excitement
Of being around you
The evenings bring you to me
So they're my favorite
The nights take you away from me
So they're sleepless

Come meet my pillow some day
For it knows the tale of our love
It may melt away in your hands
For its holding tears since months now

And, finally, she found him
He brushed his fingers through her bruises to tell her she would never fight another battle alone
He loves, unconditional and selfless, and she is awestruck
Every day, he makes her believe in love
The kind she only dreamt of

She's made up of fire
He's her fuel
She's fierce
He keeps her going
She's passionate
He's her passion
She's full of love
He's her warmth
She fights the world
And he's her strength

He doesn't just complete her, he enhances her
In every way
He loved her when nobody could
He's fire to her soul, water to her thirst
He's the flame that keeps her alive
He's put back her broken pieces and oh, so beautifully
He understands her silence and watches her dream
He puts life in her bad days
And stars in her sleepless nights

You, are like my Bombay rain
You turned up in my life least expectedly and yet most wantedly
You poured in so much love I didn't know how to handle
You soothe like the rain and bring in an unmatchable joy
And I found the moon whilst looking for the stars

You are everything a girl dreams of
You are everything a woman wants to grow old with
You are the beat in my heart
The spark in my eyes
You are my first rain
My New year winter
My morning sunshine
My midnight moon
You are the sky that makes me soar higher
And the ground that holds me
You are my noise
You are my silence
You are my love

The way I love you
I feel
I never did really love before

The long road journey
The old songs
The emptiness of parting from you until we meet again
Your fragrance in me
The lingering memories
The cold winds that remind me of you
The moon that follows me
And also stays back with you
My body with me
And my soul, I left it back with you

How, I wish, this path takes me back to you
And the time stops when I see you
And my eyes stop blinking when they look into yours
You hold me in your arms
And I forget the world
How, I wish, this path takes me back to you

The sight of you waving goodbye as the wheels roll
Teary eyes playing memories of a short meet in a flash
My eyes looking for you till the road curves
And my heart sinking in till I see you again
Such is the love you've made me fall in

Every day I battle within myself
To love you less
To remember you lesser
And every day I fail
Miserably
And I somehow love this failure
For I love you more
And miss you even more

You said my love for you is crazy
You don't even know the extent of my love for you yet
My poetry may tell you a fraction of it
But I don't know if you'd read it

And then I shall rise
Above the flames
Leaving behind your memories
And rebuild my heart
And fence it with bars

You know while I write all these poetry for you
I can see your face – smiling
Oh that charming smile, the one which took away my heart
And still does
And how my eyes get locked into yours
And I just can't look away
For Your eyes speak more than you do

I don't believe in coincidences
Our meeting was destined
My love for you was destined
But my love for you is my thing
You don't have to love me back
I wish you would, but I know you don't
I will live with my love for you
And let you live with your indifference towards me

www.ingramcontent.com/pod-product-compliance
Lightning Source LLC
LaVergne TN
LVHW041133150826
845673LV00007B/2301

* 9 7 9 8 8 9 2 7 7 6 5 1 6 *